from black & white to colour

Richard Wilkins

First Print 1999
Second Print 2003

Published by cantecia
PO Box 454   Northampton   NN4 0GJ

ISBN 0 9528198 3X

Illustrations Steff Suter
Additional illustrations David Suter

Cover design by Richard Wilkins
Printed by Candor Print, Northampton

DEDICATION

To my three sons
Carl, Lee and Ollie.

Even when you were small

I looked up to you.

INTRODUCTION

The only thing that can truly limit your life is your lack of vision. When you change how you look at life, everything in life will change, it has to.

But we limit our vision with our doubts and fears which we use to build high walls around our lives. We build them to protect us. Instead they imprison us.

Then one day, probably when you least expect it, something special will come into your life. It will be like someone lands a balloon within the confines of your walls, they will smile and say, '... *I have seen beyond your walls, there is so much more than here, come and see...*'.

You won't believe your eyes. From this new point of view, you'll see your life through your potential, you'll see beyond your fears, beyond your doubts... beyond the walls.

Just a glimpse of the bigger picture will be enough for your life to expand into a new awareness. Instantly, with-out effort, your world will change...
... from black and white to colour.

◆

Let this book be your balloon, use it as a catalyst to see your life from a different point of view, then your world could change ....

from black and white to colour...

A marker of your progress
is when the same book
has a different meaning.

Please believe these words

Before I couldn't always be with you,
but that's all changed now,
you see, there's no time in heaven,
which means I can never be without you,
so - I'm always with you.
I'm with you now, as you read these words.

I can see things much more clearly than before.
I can see that the biggest part of us always remains in heaven
and only a tiny consciousness comes to earth.
So you see, the bigger part of you is here, with me, now.

It's not so easy to see me as before, but that's OK,
it's only because you're looking through
that tiny earth bound consciousness.
I was brought back because I was needed
to be closer to God and to you.

Heaven is even better than I thought it would be,
you see, it isn't a place, it's a feeling.
Imagine the most wonderful feeling - ever,
multiply it by the biggest number - ever.
Well that's where I live now.

Heaven is far too wonderful to be a place,
things can happen to places,
they're a bit like bodies,
that's why we don't need them here.

It's OK if you doubt what I'm saying -
it's just that there's no doubt in heaven.
If you're wondering why I talk as if you're not with me,
it's only because I'm talking to that tiny earth bound part of you,
and when that tiny part is ready to be released,
you'll know then what I know now.

Please don't hurry to be with me - you already are.
We have eternity, I can see it, it's so wonderful.
The rest of your life could seem long,
but remember, it's only a tiny consciousness in eternity.

Allow yourself to grieve - it's natural.
Allow yourself to doubt - it's natural.
Remember, I'm always with you - it's natural.

The pain you feel, I understand,
but know your tears are not needed for me,
how can they be when I'm standing in heaven next to you?
All our good times are not gone,
I'm in them still, and you're with me.

Please believe me, no stranger wrote these words - our love did.
Now there are no good-byes, no farewells,
how can there be when you're here, with me now?
Just as I am with you.

So I'll wait with you, until you like me are freed,
freed from that tiny, tiny consciousness called life.
Until then, I ask just one thing of you,
please believe these words.

A tiny tin of paint

Take a tiny tin of paint.
Pop off the lid.
Dip your finger in.
Now walk around your home
and flick the paint everywhere.
Take it to work,
flick it on everyone,
especially flick it on all those you love.
Whatever is leftover,
flick over yourself.

Now try to see a problem
as a tiny tin of paint.

If you were a miracle
who would you call on?
Someone who didn't believe in you
or someone who invited you in?

'There'

These are the writings of my own crude hand,
to tell a tale of a promised land.
It's not of the bible, nor of the Lord,
It's not round the corner, and it isn't abroad.

It's a place you can't see, no matter how hard you stare,
I speak to you of the place known as 'There'.
So what's the riddle of how I write
of a strange land that's away and out of sight?

Well listen my friend, pull up a chair,
while I tell you what I know of a place known as 'There'.
Looking for 'There' can have a high cost
as searching for 'There' is further lost.

How many times have you heard people say,
'I don't know when, but I'll get 'There' one day'.
Stop now and search your heart,
can you honestly say you've never taken part?

Be honest with me if you dare,
have you never once thought, *'Oh I'll get 'There'.*
So off we all go to solve life's mess,
just one problem there is no address.

It's madness itself, for how hard you strive,
with no destination you can never arrive.
I beg of you now heed what I say,
It's only my pain shows me the way.

I hear you say *'I know of such pain'*
but how can this be, when you are still sane?
I didn't listen, I hadn't a care,
the one thing I knew was, I'd get 'There'.

'There' I was with so many toys,
A mansion, fast car, a wife and three boys.
Possessions and people classed in the same verse,
but there's the truth, Oh God it's perverse.

If only I'd listened to my wife's pleading,
then perhaps I'd have noticed my internal bleeding.
My family went, I gave them a share,
you can do that you see, when you're almost 'There'.

You'll never find ' There' on the outside,
you won't do it this way, though many have tried.
So perhaps now you can understand,
you have what you want in the palm of your hand.

Now you can be 'There' just by reading this rhyme,
you see 'There' is here, it was, all the time.

Break free from your doubts
and allow your life to expand
into your potential.

Imagine

Imagine if we spent as much effort
on how we think
as we do on how we look.

Imagine if we spent as much effort
giving our time
as we do selling it.

Imagine if we spent as much effort
appreciating
as we do taking for granted.

Imagine if we spent as much effort
enjoying our dreams
as we do struggling to create realities.

Imagine if we spent as much effort
loving ourselves
as we do trying to find someone to love us.

Imagine if we spent as much effort
on what we like
as we do on what we don't.

Imagine if we spent as much effort
letting go
as we do holding on.

Imagine if we spent as much effort
enjoying the idea of heaven
as we do fearing the threat of death.

Imagine the life we'd have.

The Rusty Old Wheel

This short tale is how I feel,
about my Mum and the Rusty Old Wheel.
The hub of the wheel is what Mum was you see,
we were the spokes, my family and me.

There are many spokes that criss cross in a wheel,
just like a big family - don't you see it's so real?
At the rim of the wheel the spokes are apart,
yet so close at the hub, where they all start.

We all stayed together, whatever the pace,
like the spokes of a wheel, we all had our place.
There were times when the wheel travelled bumpy ground,
but the hub held the spokes as the wheel went round.

A central point, where all the spokes meet,
at the hub of the wheel, the spokes fit so neat.
But hubs have bearings that age and wear out,
with no hub to hold them, spokes rattle about.

Though still fixed at the rim, what could you expect?
The spokes lost the place where they used to connect.
Our hub for us, we could never replace,
now our wheel's slowed right down - lost it's old pace.

So listen all you spokes, won't you learn from me?
Cherish those hubs, they're so special you see.
For there are many spokes to be found in a wheel,
but just the one hub - now you know how I feel.

Show me the Way

Show me the way
I need to help my friend,
I have to find the special faith
only you can send.

Show me the way
Don't let me fight alone,
I need to draw the sword now
set deep within the stone.

Show me the way
Please try and hear my call,
give me the strength to carry her
should my dear friend fall.

Help me to find the words
I feel, but need to say,
not for me, just for her,
please show me the way.

Accept a heart is like an egg
and love is the chick within.
Now you know
why our hearts get broken.

Progress

I can see real progress, I'll leave the doom for others,
I want to squeeze the best from my sisters and my brothers.

I see it in kids faces, smiles now replace the tears,
never so in photos of kids from older years.

Healers everywhere now, not so, when I was small,
just countries split in two by a concrete wall.

Lands we once invaded, we now help with aid,
from ancestors who took, the pipe of peace we've made.

Doctors heal diseases, old folk live so much longer.
Olympic records smashed by bones now so much stronger.

The Church once filled with fear, now people fill with kindness,
a dog now helps the man who once struggled with his blindness.

Hands that once held swords are now gripped to the pen,
they write so it won't happen like it did back then.

The trenches are all empty gone the massive price we paid,
so let's celebrate ourselves and the progress that we've made.

The only thing that keeps a hurtful memory alive
is choosing to think it.

What has already happened
can only ever be
as good as your thoughts of it.

What has not yet happened
can only ever be
as good as your thoughts of it.

There is no gap between
the future and the past, therefore,
everything
can only ever be
as good as your thoughts of it.

Appreciation is like sunshine on your life.
Everything suddenly becomes brighter.

Richard Wilkins is my name

My mind searched through ten thousand faces,
with Eric Clapton I'd swap places.
He's been through life, he's found out
Eric Clapton, he knows what it's about.

If I was Eric Clapton I could score.
If I was Eric Clapton, could I want more?
I'd have fame, fortune and the acclaim,
if Eric Clapton was my name

….It was later that day when my friend said
poor Eric Clapton's son was dead.
The window was open while his son was playing,
what happened next goes without saying.

I've three healthy sons and now I can see
why Eric Clapton wishes he was me.

A river cannot flow
unless it has a fall

I'm sorry I can't stay

I'm sorry I can't stay
He gives a fleeting kiss,
he doesn't have the time now.
It never used to be like this.

I'm sorry I can't stay
The golf's already booked.
She eats the meal alone
that for him she cooked.

I'm sorry I can't stay
She says 'for heavens sake',
as he asks the kids to save him
a piece of birthday cake.

I'm sorry I can't stay
I said I'd meet the lads.
She goes down to the park,
sees kids out with their Dads.

I'm sorry I can't stay
He's too busy making money,
He says 'go buy yourself a present,
you deserve one honey'.

I'm sorry I can't stay
Though he knows she'd love a chat,
we'll discuss it later…
'now where did I put my hat'.

I'm sorry I can't stay
Although he can see she's hurt,
from a smudge of lipstick
she found upon his shirt.

The note she left was short,
'I've found a better way,
the kids and I have left
I'm sorry I can't stay'.

The man who owns much
and appreciates little,
will *always* be poorer
than the man who owns little
and appreciates much.

Desire digs the holes
it then gets us to fill.

My friend death

Death lives all around me
for all who live will die,
regardless I don't fear death,
here are my reasons why...

Death you are a friend
a comfort that's so real,
when pain and illness overcomes
you show us how to heal.

Still so many curse you
you're so little understood,
one day they'll see the truth
that you're only role is good.

Parents see the child as stolen
as your caring arms unfold,
your good is lost to tears
as their child for them you hold.

So gentle is your way
heaven can't be cruel,
it's only ignorance of man
that makes him his own fool.

In good health your name's not spoken
it's as if you don't exist,
so is it any wonder death
the good you do is missed?

You are the door to heaven
one day they'll see your splendour,
never as the taker
always as Gods sender.

You walk with birth as one
loved ones passed live safe with you,
you show us to the light
when this test called life is through.

All who wrongly fear you now
one day will understand,
as in heaven they are greeted
led safely by your hand.

Emotionally bankrupt:
...people who *spend* time
disliking themselves and
refuse to accept compliments
paid to them...

Don't put corks in bottles

Many folk have stored away
things they never said,
not saying how they truly felt,
they put a cork in the bottle instead.

But bottled feelings aren't like wine
with age they don't mature,
a bitter taste is all you'll get
on that you can be sure.

Some folks have many subjects
on which they'll never talk,
then resentment turns to anger
as they use another cork.

So don't put corks in bottles
better let those feelings flow,
for the feelings that can't hurt you
are the ones that you've let go.

Special People

I'd gone to help a friend
he helps them every week.
They struggle just to talk.
Me? I'm at my peak.

Their smiles flash everywhere
so many come my way,
what we only think
the special people say.

Hugs are out in plenty
reserve is not their style,
my inner voice, it whispered,
'Stop and learn a while'.

'A sports day' it was billed,
I helped them walk the race,
the only thing that ran
were tears upon my face.

Not for them I cried,
the tears were all for me,
*the tear that stings the most
is the one which helps us see.*

They thought that I had helped them
instead they had helped me,
I'm so thankful for that tear
that one that helped me see.

Many say it's important
to win the race.
Others say,
'What race?'

Lesson of the blue coloured bottle

A dad and his son of six years young
in search of treasure went,
neither had a notion
of what they would be sent.

A wonderful blue coloured bottle
shone brightly through the brook,
a gentle pull to free it
was simply all it took.

In awe they marvelled their treasure
both were on a high,
the value of a time like this
no millionaire can buy.

For hours they polished that bottle
it shone brightly like a star,
it's times like this we give a child
reminds us who we are.

Excitement flooded in,
now, the treasure they could show.
The dad looked at his son and sighed,
why do we have to grow?

But just around the corner
old tragedy was lurking,
the bubble was about to pop
on the magic they'd been working.

Whilst trying to be so careful
clumsiness crept in,
they were about to find their treasure
was only wafer thin.

It shattered when it hit the floor
tears now replaced the joy,
their treasure lost forever,
a Dad's heart goes out to his boy.

But real magic was released
just as that bottle shattered,
you see they had to lose what they had loved
to find what really mattered.

Yes, their treasure had now left them,
but what of the special time they'd had?
The adventure of the blue coloured bottle,
for the little boy and his dad.

You see although they'd lost the thing they'd loved,
at least they'd had it for a while.
As the Dad explained this moral
tears turned to a smile.

If you think you've lost a thing you loved
because it's in the past,
remember that blue coloured bottle
and all you've loved will last.

Stay open to the possibility
and hope will always fill your life.

Where I stand now

I look at you from where I stand now.

Where I stand now is paradise,
you call it heaven.

One day you will stand where I stand now.
Then you will look at those, where you stand now
and you will know what wonders await them.

Just as I know what certain wonders await you,
where I stand now.

Rock Bottom

You pushed me off....
that I would fly.

You gave me pain....
that I would heal.

You stopped me talking....
that I would listen.

You gave me fear....
that I would pray.

You took my pride....
that I would be humble.

You gave me betrayal....
that I would know forgiveness.

You took my beliefs....
that I would know knowing.

You took my job....
that I would have time to think.

You showed me poverty....
that I would find real wealth.

You showed me death....
that I would understand heaven.

You gave me darkness....
that I would shine.

Thank you

To some hurdles are barriers.
To others they're a form of exercise.

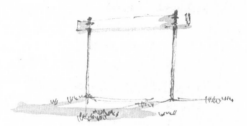

I know you'll make it through

You try to get some sleep
but night time magnifies.
Things that troubled you by day
at night time grow in size.

Awful sweaty sheets,
you wake with such a start,
a marathon you feel you've run
with such a pounding heart.

People offer you advice
you know that they're sincere,
but words that leave their mouth
rarely reach your ear.

And what about the stomach
suddenly in free fall,
it makes legs turn to jelly
so you have to crawl.

A brave face you wear for others
as life of course goes on,
but it's hard to eat a meal
when all appetite has gone.

Friendships you once valued
problems can erode,
than share a troubled path with you
many cross the road.

Some say, 'anything you need now?'
Don't you think it's funny -
as you watch them turn and run
when you ask to borrow money.

You make that fateful statement
'it can't get any worse',
then of course it does
so you go into reverse.

But I couldn't write these words
unless I'd once felt like you,
so these words come from experience,
...I know you'll make it through.

Someone who spent their life
excited and full of optimism
about things that might have happened,
but never did,
would die as they had lived,
excited and full of optimism.

My ship must sail the tide.....

It's time for me to go
and leave worldly things behind.
I need to set the sails,
those who seek, will surely find.

It's time to raise the anchor now.
My ship must sail the tide.
But don't be sad for me my friends,
I sail to another side....

The love that we have known
has guided me along my way,
my body I must leave now,
but my love will always stay.

Be happy for me please!
For I feel not a single fear.
I do not sail alone,
angels help me steer.

The voyage for me has now begun,
more wondrous than I've known.
But in your heart, I'll always live,
so we'll never be alone.

Real Wealth

Imagine someone that you love,
dies suddenly today.
Think of how you'd feel,
and the things you'd meant to say.

All the money in the world,
you'd give to bring them home.
*You see, the wealth you want,
you already own.*

A tribute of love

You are the best friend I've ever had.

What I tell you no others know.

Your dreams are my aims.

You are the brother and sister I wanted as a child.

After I have listened to others for advice,
it is you I always come to.

You are my walking, talking church,
for there is no holier place on earth
than when I am in your presence.

Your understanding is my encouragement.

Your sacrifice is my gain, my gain is your reward.

Your laughter is your happiness said aloud for others to share.

Your wisdom offers clarity to my confusion.

Your ability to compromise is the reason for my success.

Your inability at times to see your own achievements,
is merely because I have not held the mirror still enough.

Your ability to see good in small things makes them big.

You will know these words well,
for your love lives in the heart that sent them.

Much good is missed,
not because it didn't happen,
but because it wasn't noticed
when it did.

Spring is here, where is Jane?

Spring is here,
where is Jane?
So much learned
from so much pain.

Does she see the flowers?
Does she feel the breeze?
Does she touch the blossom
so fresh upon the trees?

Does she hear me speak of her
telling all that we were taught,
that she really won the battle,
for which she bravely fought?

Does she help me whilst I'm writing
trying hard to understand?
Does she guide the pen
held tight within my hand?

Does she walk beside me
as I walk the streets alone?
Is she with me as I ask
these questions on my own?

There is one thing I'm sure of,
that stands exempt from doubt.
You taught me through your dying Jane,
just what living's all about.

Appreciation

I want to love you now,
I want to appreciate and
never take our love for granted.

I want to love you now,
and thank God for your birth
and see all else you do as a bonus to my life.

I want to love you now,
not after making up from some fall out,
but in the middle of that fall out.

I want to love you now,
whilst I am able to reach out
and feel your fingers curl around my hand.

I want to love you now,
and let both our tears of joy and sorrow flow
as a single river of understanding.

I want to love you now,
enough to notice a single strand of your hair
that waves out to me on a windy day.

I want to love you now,
even when you're too busy
to notice me loving you.

I want to love you now,
not over tear stained photos
of good times we once had.

I want to love you now,
not because of painful memories
trying to escape a broken heart.

I want to love you now,
not from regret of what once was
and is no more.

I want to love you now,
not through the grief of death,
but in the time we have today.

Not some day too late,
I want to appreciate you now.

The Secret of a tidy life

If your desk is in a clutter
and much of your life needs filing
and there are things you'd like to sort
but that in-tray keeps on piling.

Are there times you nearly catch up
but there's just so much to do?
Perhaps you blame the system?
As it's the system, never you!

In-trays, out-trays, good days bad days
Do you feel you'll never win?
If you want the secret to a tidy desk
…just use the rubbish bin!

Changing your point of view
is far easier than changing
what you view.

Intuition is when the real you
gives your personality advice.

A child speaks out from heaven

Although you think I've gone
and you feel your hearts are breaking,
you think I've left you both
in a world you see as taking.

I know you feel so cheated
from the little time we had,
but this isn't what I want,
to make you feel so sad.

Please believe in me
you don't have to let me go,
I live on in your hearts
so much more than you can know.

I know it's hard to understand
but one day you'll know I'm right,
you needn't stumble in the dark
you can always use my light.

Please know that I'm still with you
and that all these words are true.
You once looked after me,
now I'm looking after you....

Importance

Importance doesn't come with things,
we attach it.

That's why things so important to others,
are not so important to us.

Important things take up most of our lives.

Few people do what they want,
they do what they think is important.

When we look back and remember good times,
were we chasing after things of importance?

Things we consider important require calculators.
things we need can be counted on one hand,

Nothing of importance can be taken to heaven,
still we use up our lives collecting things of importance.

How much of your life,
has been filled with things you really wanted to do
and how much has been spent on things of importance?

To find how important, important things are.
Just ask yourself...
How many things can I remember today,
that were *so* important this time last week?...

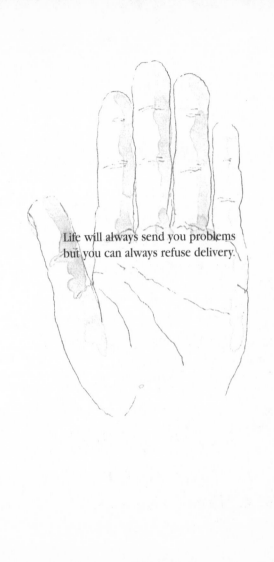

Life will always send you problems
but you can always refuse delivery.

Know this

Know this:
There is nothing, nothing,
that is stronger than the light of love.

We have been sent to show you your light.
We are from a place where all things are possible,
remember - all things.

There, burns the brightest flame of all.
It is the flame that never flickers, ever.
This same flame illumes in you, we see it, clearly.

Know this:
No illness, no person, no situation, no death, nothing,
can ever extinguish this light,
It is immortal, it is eternal, it is yours.

Wherever you go, we are there with you.
No place is ever too far for us.
We are there before you, waiting, always.

You will only see us with your heart,
not your eyes.
You will only feel us with your spirit,
not your body.

We accept no boundaries no limitations,
they are man made,
we are beyond man, *trust us.*

Know this:
We will never let you fall.
For no fear, no doubt can ever equal our light.

When the door of the cupboard is opened,
does the darkness from the cupboard spill into the room
or does the light from the room spill into the cupboard?
...Light will always triumph over darkness.

We see through your body,
we see past your doubts,
we only see your light.
What surrounds or covers your light is not you.
Your light is perfect.

Who are we?
.... we are your light.

The value of Time

So what's this Time that we can't see
that ticks away for you and me.
You can't see it, touch it, nowhere to be found
you won't hear time, no not a sound.

Little girls and little boys
we buy them off with lots of toys.
But don't you think that it's a crime?
They wanted no presents, simply our time.

A silly thing, a man made measure
yet its valued greater than any lost treasure.
Still many sell their time for a wage
then time pays them back, we call it old age.

A wealthy man may have money indeed
but what good is such wealth if time is his need?
So share your time with those who call,
for such time is real wealth, and its there, for us all.

People who resist change
will always walk against the wind.

So much more in life
is what we have gone in search of,
rather that what we have stumbled upon.

Why we don't see Angels

Did you ever see the fragrance of a rose?

Did you ever see the wind that pushes clouds across the sky?

Did you ever see the perfect note of a black bird's song?

Did you ever see the tender love that touched your heart?

The human race story

Children very young
on the line are placed.
The race will soon begin
with competition they're now faced.

Grown ups urge their child to win,
so young, and on the line.
Their little hearts are pounding
waiting for the starting sign.

Then all at once it's go!
Little legs give out their best,
but the tape knows just one winner,
still we put them through the test.

Gold goes to the winner
although their effort was no more,
just their legs moved that bit faster
so they get the highest score.

It's so sad to see the children
who's legs won't move as fast,
their effort is no less
and still they come in last.

Grown ups push their kids.
Go! and win first place!
So when they too are grown ups
they can run in the human race.

The object is to leave behind
all others if you can,
to widen up the gap between you
and your fellow man.

Now it's time to change the rules
re-write the Human Race story,
encourage the fast to wait for the slow
and let kindness be the glory.

....then the human race will be won

....then the Human Race will be one

Life without adventure is boring.
Adventure without challenge is impossible.

Let Go

Let go.
Only then are you truly free.
It takes courage to let go.
What you don't let go
you must carry - everywhere.

Most people will let go
only when their burden becomes
too heavy to bear.
So the heavier the burden,
the nearer you are to letting go.

Holding on requires far more
effort than letting go.
What you have let go,
no-one can ever take from you.

To let go of the past
is to have learned from it.
Guilt, anger and bitterness
are all derived from not letting go.

Grieving is not about dying,
it's about not letting go.

No matter how stubborn you are
one day you will let go of everything
when you let go of life.

Then you will understand
that heaven isn't dying,
it's simply letting go.

The Punch and Judy Show

Happiness and unhappiness,
these two control our way.
But they're only Punch and Judy
in this game we play.

One minute we are up,
in the next one we are downed.
So just like Punch and Judy,
we go another round.

Now it's time to sit back,
and watch them from afar.
When you don't play their game,
you'll discover who they are.

You won't stop them performing,
but it's a choice to be in the cast.
So enjoy the show they put on,
and find contentment at last.

When you recognise contentment in someone,
is it someone wanting more,
or someone needing less?

The dying man

Lying in his bed alone,
dreams now fill his head,
thinking things he could have done,
and things he could have said.

Reflections of a life,
drawing rapid to it's end,
a past shown straight back to him,
he knows he can't defend.

Tears stream down his face,
from regrets that use his eyes,
so much that he can see now,
before he didn't realise.

His pillow is the sponge,
which soaks up all his tears,
he wants to turn the clock back,
with hours left, not years.

No emphasis on money,
no possessions can he take,
his only thought is people,
as the cord of life is set to break.

Where did his lifetime go?
What was it all about?
Why did he let all false things in,
and shut all real things out?

The murky view he'd had,
now was crystal clear.
It's always at this time,
when angels draw in near.

All importance fell away,
till just one thing remained.
It's said it sailed out on a tear,
as the key to life he gained.

Now of the dying man,
there's little left to say,
he simply gave a sigh,
and gently slipped away.

But that's not where it ends,
instead it's where it starts.
He gave us all a chance,
to open up our hearts.

Use these words he gave you,
the man who stands at heavens gate,
then you'll *never* have to say one day,
I left my life to late.

People who go out in search of perfection
always come back empty handed..

Wet Sand

Love is like wet sand.
It can take on any shape,
so you hold it very tight
you don't want it to escape.

Then for the best of reasons
to protect it from all harm,
you squeeze a little tighter
when love is in your palm.

But that's when things will go wrong,
sand held tightly always dries,
then it slips right through your finger tips
and blows back into your eyes.

Then wondrous shapes that used to be,
when dry, all fall apart.
Underestimate the power of sand
and the sand will break your heart.

Don't make the same mistakes as me
go build your castles in the sand,
don't squeeze what you love too tight,
don't let love slip through your hand.

Allow your enjoyment
the same freedom
as your worries.

Problems are like clouds.
They can make things darker,
but they never stay.

Faith is the line God throws to those in need.
Sadly, many allow it to slip through their fingers
just because they can't see
who is holding the other end.

Me to God

If you really love me
why do you keep allowing me to fall?

God to me

If the parent stopped the child every time it fell
the child would never learn to walk.

I love you enough to let you fall.

Elaine

I went into myself
to find these words for you,
to that special place
to where all dreams come true.

I asked why you had a body
that only moved a fraction,
why it's so hard for you to speak,
I asked them for some action.

Now I've journeyed back
with stardust in my veins,
to share what I was told
from those of other plains.

To hear these words in truth
disregard all you've been taught,
rise far above yourself
until you only live in thought.

Before this life began
you lived another life,
where you shone out like a star
where joy and love were rife.

There you were a leader
an example to the rest,
but your soul's need was to teach
so you took on the toughest test.

So you see the truth is
you are a higher being,
you're the soul that you can't see,
not the body you are seeing.

To be the most successful climber
the toughest mountain you would climb.
You see you've reached a summit
we can only hope to reach in time.

Enlightenment

I'd always used a light separate from me.
A light I could not control.
A light that would come on and go off without warning,
and often did.

One day it became very dark and stayed dark.
At Rock Bottom there is no light at the end of the tunnel,
only darkness.

After a time I became aware of a light.
This light was different, softer, somehow warmer.
Everywhere I looked, the light shone.
It didn't go out like before.
I realised it was my light.
And the more I believe in the light
the brighter it shines.

Now I am never without light.

It's easier to make your window bigger
than to make
the sun brighter.

Surely the ego has won the day
when it has convinced us
that it is wrong to say or think
good things about ourselves?

What is said is said,
what is heard is a choice.

The Humming Bird

She gazes out the window,
lives out all her fears,
she dreams of going back,
to her younger years.

He used to be so different,
so caring and so kind,
now she hardly knows him,
she fights to keep her mind.

He makes her feel so worthless,
the control goes on and on,
she used to be so sure,
now all confidence is gone.

The kids help keep her sanity,
she says that when they're older,
that's when she'll make her move,
she prays then she'll be bolder.

She panics in his company,
her aching heart gives pounding pulses,
the one that once caressed her,
now openly repulses.

He never listens to her views,
his word's the only one,
where is that man that she once knew
who used to be such fun?

She cries most on her own,
how have things got so bad?
Is it him or her she thinks,
or am I going mad?

The humming bird that used to sing,
so cruelly has been caged,
but the sun will always shine again,
when the storm has raged.

Where she found her strength from,
to this day she's not quite sure,
but the time it had to come,
when she could take no more.

He didn't think she meant it,
he still can't understand
how the humming bird could fly again,
when squeezed tight within his hand.

Since she dared to leap,
her confidence keeps growing,
she's flown away from doubt,
and settled back to knowing.

She's not frightened on her own,
she knows she'll make it through,
'Just believe in yourself' she says,
'you'll be amazed what you can do'.

Now she can't believe her joy,
after knowing so much pain,
you can cage a humming bird,
but it will always fly again.

Many more people hold back
than are held back.

Looking at the world
through rose tinted glasses
may not be the answer.
But it sure makes things
a lot prettier
until the answer comes.

It's Just Your Imagination

A voice once came to visit me.
It said, 'Trust in me'
So I did.

'See the sky bluer'
So I did.

'Hear the birds singing louder'
So I did.

'Feel the sun warmer'
So I did.

'Set free all worries'
So I did.

'Let your heart be full of love'
So I did.

'Be at last content'
And I was.

Then the voice was gone and I was back as before.

The next day the voice returned.
'How are you today?', it said.
'No better than before you first came', I snapped.
'Yesterday were you not content?'
'For a while', I said, 'Then I discovered the truth'.
'What truth', said the voice.
'That it had all been just my imagination'.
'Wonderful', said the voice, 'Now use it well!'
'Who are you?', I asked,
'Why, just your imagination', said the voice.

Don't limit the outcome
by being attached to it's source.

The Dawning

The dawning has arrived
the true awakening of light,
now is the time to know
we've lived so much in night.

No longer round the corner
not a promise to be broken,
the dawning is of now
what once slept has now awoken.

No badge you need to wear
no matter what your creed,
regardless of your church
from all fear you will be freed.

It's said you are a child of God,
then a God you have to be.
For long we've been the seed
now it's time to be the tree.

Old ways will have no place
text books turned to dust,
lessons known yet never learned
all hatred turned to trust.

Death will live with life as one
as eternity breaks through,
knowing we can't fall
no matter what we do.

As healing bonds the planet
empty hearts will fill with love,
and you'll find heaven is inside you
not in the clouds above.

This isn't what might happen
it's not open for debate,
you see the dawning has begun
…now it can never be too late.

ACKNOWLEDGMENTS

Yvonne Bell
your generosity and faith in me
allowed my dreams to become this book

Lisa and Jonathan Coward
you give and you give
I have lost count of the many different ways
you have given me kindness, encouragement & warmth

Martine Donnellan
you gave me the best Christmas present I've ever had
when you gave birth to my beautiful granddaughter, Jessica,
on Christmas Day

Colin Edwards
you have cleared the path for me and many others
you deserve the best

Suzy Greaves
your support for me has helped more people
than you will ever know

Rev. Chris Lee
you carved my words on Tessa's headstone
and you carved your name on my heart

Preethi Nair
you have given me something incredibly precious - your time

Kathy Sargeant
your generosity has provided me a home in which to live
and sanctuary for others in which to rest

Steve, Sharon & Vaughan at Candor Print
you have given me so much
so many more times than you needed

Leonora Whitfield
you made me a proud Pops for the first time
when you gave birth to my beautiful granddaughter, Olivia

Tony Wilson
your encouragement showed me the potential for this book

To Gillian
thank you for your encouragement

What's been said (and by who) about Richard and his books

Stella McCartney	'...the books brighten up my day...'
Geri Halliwell	'...these books have inspirational quotations which sort of bully you into feeling better...'
Anthea Turner	'...your books are truly inspirational, especially on the down days we all have, I've read every page.'
Richard Branson	'...how delightful...'
Daily Mail	'...thoughts which make you think about what's important in life...'
New Woman	'...a must for a stressed out soul...'
Dr Bernie Seigel	'...I heartily endorse your book, I know the wisdom of pain and passion, and you have found it...'
Robert Holden	'...This little book of gems can add sparkle to your life. Read and look carefully...'
Revd Chris Lee	'... thank you for all you have given through your books, they're a constant source of strength and sensibility...'
British Reflexology Association	'...these pocket sized books are filled with a wealth of advice..'
British Telecom	'...nothing but praise for the pertinence of the book's contents...
Reading Post	'...deep and humourous...'
Looking Good Magazine	'...he draws from experiences which sound incredibly far fetched, but really happened to him..'
All About Making Money	'...full of inspirational thoughts and inspiring snippets... sign posts readers can use to guide their lives...'
Success Now	'...if ever you needed evidence that success - real success is not just about making money, then this story will convince you...'

About the Author

Richard was shown a glimpse of the bigger picture when he found himself alone, terrified and broke on Rock Bottom after crashing from a millionaire in a mansion to a bankrupt in a bedsit.

Since his world changed from black and white to colour, he has become the UK's most successful author in his field and is now reaching millions of people through his books, talks and TV appearances with his message of hope and optimism.

Richard's works:

150 Ways to make your life Ten out of Ten ISBN 09528198 05
The first book of quotations.

The Yellow Book ISBN 0952819813
The second book of quotations.

Mental Tonic ISBN 0952819880
The third book of quotations.

Collection Box ISBN 0952819848
All three quotation books in a presentation case.

Inner Nutshell-Cards ISBN 0952819821
60 inspirational cards.

When God Asks ISBN 0952819864
A pocket sized book of thought provoking questions.

Forever Inspired A six CD collection
Richard guides you through his unique philosphy
in a six part programme.

For up to date information and further details of Richard's works, live events and to purchase products, visit www.foreverinspired.co.uk

To be placed on our e-mailing list for news, events and latest releases, email: info@foreverinspired.co.uk

www.foreverinspired.co.uk